The Madchester Quiz Book

100 Trivia Questions to test your fan knowledge!

This quiz has 100 entertaining trivia questions about the Madchester scene, circa 1989-91

I've tried to include a really good mix of easy questions, harder questions, and in a few cases, extremely tough ones. Can't have you getting 100% now can I?

Some sets of questions are multiple choice, and some are open answer. This is deliberate so that whether you're a new fan or an expert, there's something for your level.

You'll be asked questions on a wide range of topics surrounding Manchester music.
You'll be quizzed on band members, songs, albums, and a bunch of other trivia you didn't know existed!

Just a quick note:
This is meant to be a fun and entertaining book, not a test!
Take it easy, don't stress, and don't use the internet unless you're really, really stuck!

Have fun!
DJ Moto Noir

Disclaimer

Cover photo courtesy of Leah Thomas

Round 1

Questions 1 – 10

Starting off with a multiple choice format and some easier questions to get you into the swing of things!

The answers can be found after the questions, before the title page for the next round.

1. What was the name of the Manchester nightclub started
    by Factory Records and New Order?

        A. Fascination Street
        B. The Fascination
        C. Hacienda

2. Which drug was credited with driving the Madchester
    scene?

        A. Ecstasy
        B. Heroin
        C. Marijuana

3. The Summers of 1988 and 1989 were given a nickname
    based on the San Francisco scene of the late Sixties. What
    was the name?

        A. Flower Time
        B. Second Summer of Love
        C. Summer of Love

4. The Madchester fave Pacific State reached number 10 in
    the UK charts. But who recorded it?

        A. Pacific
        B. Ocean Colour Scene
        C. 808 State

5. Tim Burgess is the lead singer of which band?

        A. James
        B. Charlatans
        C. Soup Dragons

6. Which band's massive self-titled album was released
   on the Silvertone label?

   A. Electronic
   B. Stone Roses
   C. New Order

7. "Telephone Thing" pushed which veteran band firmly
   into the Madchester scene??

   A. The Fall
   B. The Farm
   C. New Order

8. Which British film released in 2002 covered the
   Madchester scene and Tony Wilson in particular?

   A. Once Upon a Time in the Midlands
   B. Hit the North
   C. 24 Hour Party People

9. Name the album that contained the singles Step On,
   Kinky Afro, and Loose Fit?

   A. Pills 'n' Thrills and Bellyaches
   B. Some Friendly
   C. Bummed

10. Which Madchester classic was remixed by Fatboy Slim
    in 2003 and reached number 19 in the UK charts, just
    failing to pip the original version's number 18 in the
    charts 12 years earlier

    A. Step On
    B. Sit Down
    C. Can You Dig It?

Answers for Round 1

A1. Of course, the club was The Hacienda

A2. The new availability of ecstasy drove the scene.

A3. The answer is B. The period was known as The Second Summer of Love.

A4. 808 State had a hit with Pacific State, also known as Pacific, Pacific 202, 303, 707 or whichever mix you are listening to!

A5. Tim is the lead singer of The Charlatans!

A6. The debut album by The Stone Roses "The Stone Roses" was released on Silvertone.

A7. January 1990 saw the release of the danceable Telephone Thing which became a cult classic for The Fall.

A8. 24 Hour Party People

A9. It was Pills 'n' Thrills and Bellyaches by The Happy Mondays.

A10. Strangely, the new mix of The Mock Turtles' "Can You Dig It" reached almost the same position as the 1991 original.

Round 2

Questions 11 – 10

So how did you do on that first round? Quite well I hope. Just in case you found it too easy, this round is open answer!

As before, the answers can be found after the questions, before the title page for the next round.

11. Factory Records and The Hacienda owner Tony Wilson was a presenter for which British TV company?

12. What was the name of Northside's only album?

13. Which band containing an early Stone Roses member had a summer 1990 hit with Box Set Go?

14. Which band contained members of New Order and The Smiths, and collaborated with members of The Pet Shop Boys to pen a Madchester dance classic?

15. Whose debut album Some Friendly reached number 1 in the UK album charts and took only 3 days to be certified gold?

16. Who was scheduled to produce the first Stone Roses album but commitments with his own Manchester band meant it was given to John Leckie?

17. The Stone Roses played an outdoor concert to 27000 people on May 27th, 1990. What was the name of the venue?

18. Bez was percussionist and dancer for which Madchester band?

19. Who is the lead singer of James?

20. Inspiral Carpets' distinct organ sound was provided by which Oldham musician?

Answers for Round 2

A11. Tony was a presenter for Granada Television, the ITV franchise holder for the north west of England.

A12. The only album Northside released before the downfall of Factory Records and their subsequent split was Chicken Rhythms.

A13. The High, featuring guitarist Andy Couzens, had a UK top 30 hit with Box Set Go.

A14. Bernard Sumner of New Order and Johnny Marr of The Smiths formed Electronic, and collaborated with Neil Tennant and Chris Lowe to release the single "Getting Away With It"

A15. It was the debut album by The Charlatans.

A16. New Order's Peter Hook was originally in line to produce the MDCR classic, "The Stone Roses".

A17. Spike Island, a park in Widnes, Cheshire.

A18. The Happy Mondays.

A19. Tim Booth.

A20. Clint Boon.

Round 3

Questions 21 – 30

How was round 2?

Bearing in mind those were a little bit harder, the next round is going to be multiple choice again.

In fact, this is how we're going to carry on, alternating between the two kinds of questions each round from now on. That way if you're getting behind you can have a good old guess at the multiple choice questions and maybe catch up!

21. Tony Wilson presented a television show on Granada profiling indie bands. What was it called?

A. The Old Grey Whistle Test
B. So It Goes
C. Go!

22. What logo became a symbol of the Second Summer of Love?

A. A sheep
B. A smiley face
C. The peace sign

23. Which New York musicians released a break mix of 808 State's Pacific on The Tommy Boy Mixes in 1990?

A. Beastie Boys
B. Musto and Bones
C. Grandmaster Flash and Melle Mel

24. Who was the lead singer of New Fast Automatic Daffodils?

A. Andy Spearmint
B. Andy Spearpoint
C. Andy Pierpoint

25. Which Madchester band contained the older brother of actor and comedian Steve Coogan?

A. The Bridewell Taxis
B. The Happy Mondays.
C. The Mock Turtles

26. British DJ John Peel's Festive Fifty poll for 1990 included Madchester classics Step On, The Only One I Know, and Beast Inside, amongst others. But which other Manchester song was Number 1?

A. Bill Is Dead
B. Perfume (All on You)
C. She Bangs the Drums

27. What was Johnny Marr's name at birth?

A. John Mayer
B. John Martin Maher
C. Jonathan Marr

28. The Gay Traitor, Kim Philby, and Hicks were all what kind of establishments in Manchester?

A. Clothing shops
B. Bars
C. Record shops

29. Northside had a minor UK hit with which song?

A. Take That
B. Take 5
C. You Blown It

30. Clyde Stubblefield's "Funky Drummer" drum pattern was the base for which 11 minute song?

A. The Stone Roses' Elephant Stone
B. The Stone Roses' Fool's Gold
C. New Order's Elegia

Answers for Round 3

A21. Tony presented So It Goes.

A22. The smiley face became the symbol of SSOL after being seen on Ibiza rave posters

A23. It's B, Musto and Bones

A24. Andy Spearpoint

A25. The Mock Turtles lead singer is Martin Coogan, older brother of Steve.

A26. The annual fan's poll picked Bill Is Dead by The Fall as the Festive Fifty number one in 1990.

A27. The Smith's guitarist was born John Martin Maher

A28. They were all bars in The Hacienda!

A29. It was Take 5.

A30. The classic drum pattern was the basis for Fool's Gold

Round 4

Questions 31 – 40

Okay, on we go. You know how it works by now!

31. Tasty Fish was the debut single of a band called "The Other Two". Who were the two members and which much, much, much bigger band were they in?

32. What was the preferred brand of baggy jeans worn by the Madchester culture?

33. Graham Massey, Gerald Simpson and Martin Price formed which Madchester band?

34. Which Madchester band had a monster UK hit with the song "Perfume / All on You".

35. Famed for his New Order work, who produced Box Set Go by The High?

36. The Only One I Know was not The Charlatan's debut single. What was?

37. Stone Roses guitarist John Squire went on to form which "hippocampus" band?

38. Which song contains the chorus "I couldn't bring myself to hate you as I'd like"?

39. After multiple line-up changes, who said "If it's me and your granny on bongos, it's The Fall"

40. "He's Gonna Step on you Again" is a line from a top MDCR song, but it's a cover. The original was by whom?

Answers for Round 4

A31. Stephen Morris and Gillian Gilbert of New Order.

A32. Joe Bloggs!

A33. 808 State.

A34. Paris Angels!

A35. It was classic New Order producer Martin Hannett.

A36. Their first single was Indian Rope

A37. The Seahorses

A38. It's in the chorus of "I am the Resurrection" by The Stone Roses.

A39. Easy one! Mark E. Smith.

A40. Ahhhh. The Happy Mondays song "Step On" is a cover! The original was by John Kongos.

Round 5

<u>Questions 41 – 50</u>

Multiple choice again.

41. "What For" was a single from which big MDCR album?

A. Strip-Mine
B. Laid
C. Seven

42. Which musician was the only ever present throughout the entire history of Inspiral Carpets?

A. Graham Lambert
B. Craig Gill
C. Clint Boon

43. Which country music star's publishing company sued New Order over similarities in the song Run?

A. Merle Haggard
B. John Denver
C. Johnny Cash

44. In 1993, members of Ruthless Rap Assassins, Happy Mondays, and Paris Angels formed which band?

A. Freebass
B. Bad Lieutenant
C. Black Grape

45. Who played Martin Hannett in the film 24 Hour Party People?

A. Andy Serkis
B. Elijah Wood
C. Orlando Bloom

46. Which 808 State album was influential in the development
of the Madchester scene?

A. Newbuild
B. Pills 'n' Thrills and Bellyaches
C. Ex:el

47. Which musician recorded an acoustic version of Paris
Angels' Perfume / All on You on a 6 track EP release?

A. Mark Gardener of Ride
B. Andy Bell of Ride
C. Andy Bell of Erasure

48. Name the keyboardist who perfected The Charlatans'
famous Hammond organ sound?

A. Clint Boon
B. Rob Collins
C. Tony Rogers

49. What was the first single released from The Stone Roses
second album, Second Coming?

A. Love Spreads
B. This is the One
C. Ten Storey Love Song

50. The drums on The Charlatans' "Then" are inspired by a
clip from which classic Hip Hop album?

A. De La Soul's Three Feet High and Rising
B. Boogie Down Productions' By All Means Necessary
C. Public Enemy's Yo! Bum Rush The Show

Answers for Round 5

A41. What For is from Strip-Mine

A42. Graham Lambert was the guitarist from start to finish.

A43. It was John Denver's publication company that claimed Run was too similar to "I'm Leaving on a Jet Plane". Consequently, a writing credit for John Denver was added to the song.

A44. Shaun Ryder and Bez of the Happy Mondays; Kermit, Psych and Ged Lynch from the Ruthless Rap Assassins, and Wags from the Paris Angels formed Black Grape.

A45. Gollum actor Andy Serkis.

A46. 808 State's debut, Newbuild.

A47. Andy Bell of Ride.

A48. Original keyboardist Rob Collins.

A49. It was Love Spreads, reaching number two in the UK charts.

A50. According to Tim Burgess, drummer Jon Brookes adapted the beat after hearing it on Three Feet High and Rising.

Round 6

<u>Questions 51 – 60</u>

Questions getting harder now, I think.
A little more detailed, perhaps.

51. The catchy single What Do You Want From Me was a
single by which band containing a New Order
member?

52. Which DJ was hugely influential in the production
and mixing of Happy Mondays' classic album, Pills 'n'
Thrills and Bellyaches?

53. Which James album was widely criticized as a
departure into "stadium rock"?

54. Which Madchester album cover is a garden statue on a
pink background?

55. Who were Tony Wilson's 3 original partners in
Factory Records?

56. Gerald Simpson of 808 State left to form his own
project. What was it called?

57. What was the name of the first New Fast Automatic
Daffodils album that contained their most well-known
song Big?

Now, three questions about James' support bands

58. Which massive band supported James on their Spring
1988 tour?

59. Which iconic Madchester band supported James on
their Autumn 1988 tour?

60. And which band supported James on their Spring
1989 tour?

Answers for Round 6

A51. Monaco, featuring Peter Hook and David Potts of Revenge.

A52. It was Paul Oakenfold.

A53. Seven. For example, the Chicago Tribune described it as a "soulless imitation of U2".

A54. New Order's Technique.

A55. Martin Hannett, Alan Erasmus and Rob Gretton

A56. A Guy Called Gerald.

A57. It was 1990's Pigeonhole.

A58. The Stone Roses.

A59. The Happy Mondays.

A60. Inspiral Carpets

Crazy to think that these three iconic Madchester bands all supported James!

Round 7

Questions 61 – 70

So, this is actually the most difficult part of the quiz for me. I've basically used up all the easier, introductory questions, and I'm trying not to make it too hard. But all I have left are hard questions!

At least it's multiple choice again, so you can have a guess, right?

61. Who is the only surviving original member of The
    Charlatans?

A. Martin Blunt
B. Tim Burgess
C. Mark Collins

62. Which A Guy Called Gerald tune reached number 12
    in the UK charts and helped define the Madchester
    sound?

A. Trip City
B. Voodoo Ray
C. FX

63. Alan Wren played drums for which band?

A. The La's
B. Distant Cousins
C. Stone Roses

64. Which Madchester classic was used in commercials for
    Vodafone in 2002 and 2003?

A. Step On
B. 24 Hour Party People
C. Can You Dig It?

65. Get The Message was a mellow dance hit for which
    Madchester band?

A. Monaco
B. The Other Two
C. Electronic

66. Tom Hingley replaced Stephen Holt as the lead singer
of Inspiral Carpets in 1989. From which other
Manchester band did he join?

A. Texas Toast
B. Texas
C. Too Much Texas

67. FAC275 is the catalog number for which New Order
album?

A. Technique
B. Substance
C. Brotherhood

68. The Happy Monday's lyric "You're twisting my melon
man" came from a line in Man on the Edge, a
documentary film about which American actor?

A. Andy Kaufman
B. Jack Nicholson
C. Steve McQueen

69. What was the highest position This is How it Feels by
The Charlatans reached in the UK charts?

A. Number 1
B. Top Ten
C. Top Twenty

70. Despite clearly defining the Madchester sound, the
Charlatans were actually formed in what area?

A. Birmingham area
B. Liverpool area
C. Glasgow area

Answers for Round 7

A61. Bassist Martin Blunt is the only remaining original member of The Charlatans

A62. The classic Voodoo Ray.

A63. Alan Wren is the real name of Reni of The Stone Roses.

A64. Can You Dig It by The Mock Turtles.

A65. Of course Get The Message was a classic Madchester song by Electronic.

A66. He joined from fellow Manchester band Too Much Texas

A67. That's the catalog number for Technique.

A68. The seminal Madchester lyric is from a documentary about Steve McQueen.

A69. This Is How It Feels reached number 14 in the UK charts, making it a Top Twenty hit.

A70. The Charlatans were actually from the Birmingham area, but moved to Manchester after Salford-born Tim Burgess took over vocals from Baz Ketley.

Round 8

<u>Questions 71 – 80</u>

We're closing in on the last few rounds! Are you doing alright? Hang on in there and go for it!

71. Fill in the blanks. The Madchester sound is generally considered to be made up of which four musical styles?

F___ , P_________ , G_____ , H_____

72. Which Madchester band covered an acid house version of New Order's Blue Monday called the So Hot Mix which was released on Rephlex Records in 2004?

73. Which band, whose first album was called _________ and the Family of People, featured lead vocalist Stella Grundy?

74. Gary Mounfield played bass for which band?

75. Which female singer contributed the backing vocals to Happy Monday's Step On?

76. What was the first track of the 1989 demo album released by Inspiral Carpets called Dung 4, which was re-released in 2014?

77. Which electronic act had a UK number 3 hit with Ain't No Love (Ain't No Use) before becoming the band Doves?

78. In 24 Hour Party People, Simon Pegg (Shaun of the Dead) and Rob Brydon (The Trip) played characters from which profession?

79. Which James album contained the singles How Was It For You and Come Home?

80. A remix of Happy Monday's Hallelujah by Steve Lillywhite featured female vocals by his then wife. Who was she?

Answers for Round 8

A71. The Madchester baggy sound is considered to be made up of Funk, Psychedelia, Guitar, and House.

A72. Classic acid housers 808 State.

A73. Intastella.

A74. Gary is better known as Mani, bassist for The Stone Roses.

A75. Session singer Rowetta had her vocals dubbed onto Step On, later becoming a member of the band.

A76. The first track was Keep the Circle Around.

A77. Sub Sub later became Doves.

A78. They both played journalists.

A79. The James album is Gold Mother.

A80. Steve mixed in vocals by Kirsty MacColl, his first wife.

Round 9

Questions 81 – 90

81. Whose remix of Wrote For Luck (WFL) was key in bringing the Happy Mondays into the indie dance scene?

A. Vince Clarke of Erasure
B. Andy Bell of Erasure
C. Anne Clark

82. Biting Tongues, Beach Surgeons and Hit Squad MCR are all projects of which MDCR musician?

A. Bernard Sumner
B. Shaun Ryder
C. Graham Massey

83. Jayne Gill was a female vocalist with which Madchester band?

A. Paris Angels
B. New Order
C. Happy Mondays

84. Ian Brown of Stone Roses is famously pictured wearing a t-shirt comprising burnt banknotes. At what gig was the picture taken?

A. Blackpool Empress Aug 12, 1989
B. Heaton Park, Jun 29, 2012
C. Spike Island, May 27, 1990

85. Which Leeds act supported Happy Mondays, Inspiral Carpets and Stone Roses and had a minor hit with Spirit, thrusting them, somewhat unwittingly, into the Madchester scene?

A. Pale Saints
B. Bridewell Taxis
C. Nightmares on Wax.

86. Doreen Edwards sang lead vocals for which soul/pop band attached to the Madchester scene, that had a minor hit in 1990 with You Used to?

A.   Distant Cousins
B.   Coldcut
C.   Blue Zone

87. A lyrics question. Who "has come to take me away" and " is mine when she stitches me"?

A.   My Sugar Spun Sister
B.   She (the one who bangs the drums)
C.   The Only One in The Only One I Know

88. Which Madchester anthem contains a line about "passion fruit and holy bread"?

A.   She Bangs the Drums
B.   Step On
C.   Voodoo Ray

89. Album Art question. A purple and red collage by Anthony Frost was the artwork for which 1990 Madchester album?

A.   Extricate by The Fall
B.   Obey the Time by The Durutti Column
C.   Somewhere Soon by The High

90. What were M62, Debris and City Life?

A.   Clubs
B.   Record stores
C.   Magazines

Answers for Round 9

A81. Wrote For Luck was remixed by Vince Clarke of Erasure

A82. They are all projects of Graham Massey of 808 State.

A83 Jayne Gill was a vocalist for Paris Angels.

A84. The picture was taken at the Blackpool Empress gig, Aug 12, 1989.

A85. Leeds band The Bridewell Taxis had a minor hit with Spirit

A86. Doreen sang for Distant Cousins.

A87. The lyrics are from The Only One I know by The Charlatans

A88. " I don't feel too steady on my feet
I feel hollow I feel weak
Passion fruit and holy bread
Fill my guts and ease my head"

From She Bangs the Drums.

A89. It's Extricate. Artist Anthony Frost created the album art for many of The Fall's LPs.

A90. They were Manchester magazines that helped document the MDCR scene

Round 10

<u>Questions 91 – 99</u>

We've almost come to the end! I hope you've enjoyed the quiz.
If you have, please consider checking out some of my other band and genre trivia, and other fun gift books I write.

Please note!

Just for fun, question 100 is a little fiendish, so it has its own round all to itself following round 10.

91. Which Manchester guitarist has worked with The Stone Roses, Ian Brown, members of The Smiths, as well as Simply Red and Paul Weller, and scored the music for Playstation's Eliminator?

92. Which 808 State song samples the bass line from She's Lost Control?

93. What was the first single from Electronic's self-titled album Electronic?

94. Which Inspiral Carpets song first appeared on a flexidisc given away free with debris magazine?

95. Which four songs were on Happy Mondays' Manchester Rave On EP?

96. A remix of which James song reached number 2 in the UK Charts in 1991?

97. What was the title of the EP released by Inspiral Carpets in 1988?

98. "It takes years to find the nerve" is a lyric from which New Order song on the Technique album?

99. Which founding member of Happy Mondays passed away in July, 2022?

Answers for Round 10

A91. That would be Aziz Ibrahim!

A92. Contrique samples that bass line.

A93. The first single from that album was Get the Message.

A94. A Garage Full of Flowers.

A95. Hallelujah, Holy Ghost, Clap your Hands, and Rave On.

A96. Sit Down 1991 reached number 2 on 30th March, 1991. The original version reached number 7 in July 1989.

A97. It was the Plane Crash EP. Tracks were : Keep the Circle Around, Theme from Cow, Seeds of Doubt, Garage Full of Flowers, and 96 Tears.

A98. It's track 2, All the Way.

A99. Bassist Paul Ryder

Round 11

Question 100

The final question!

I always make this quite difficult and a bit silly, and here's why:

You've come a long way since easy question 1, so here's your reward.

The last question is always so hard, that if you get it COMPLETELY correct, it doesn't matter how badly you've done so far, I'll let you say

YOU'VE WON THE QUIZ!

But remember, you must get everyone right, and no cheating on the internet!

Good luck!

100. The following ten people all worked at The Hacienda.
In order to succeed on this question, you must match the
correct position to the individual.

Example: Tony Wilson = Owner

There are:

5 DJs,
1 Operations Manager,
1 General Manager,
1 Bar Manager
1 Female Doorperson,
1 Head Bouncer

Here's your list of personnel, good luck!

Ang Matthews
Hedd
Lolly Lomas
Little Martin
Paul Mason
Hewan Clarke
Damien Noonan
Bobby Langley
Greg Wilson
Leroy Richardson

Answer for Round 11

Here is the employee list and their positions :

Ang Matthews worked her way up to General Manager

Hedd was a DJ often on Saturday nights like "Wide"

Lolly Lomas was a muscular female doorperson

Little Martin was a DJ who now lives and works in the US.

Paul Mason was Operations Manager.

Hewan Clarke was the first resident DJ with great taste in funk and soul

Damien Noonan was the Head Bouncer

Bobby Langley was a DJ who ended up buying the DJ Booth!

Greg Wilson was a DJ famous for his funk nights

Leroy Richardson was the long time Bar Manager

The End

My Score:

____

Thank You

Thank you to Alice le Blanc, co-author of "I Love You More Than" whose weekly presence for that book spurred me to finally complete this long-standing project.

Thank you to Melangll, whose Spotify blend for 2022 became inadvertently overwhelmed with every Madchester track available.

Thank you to Shinobi whose playlists always make me smile and remind me to check my Twitch!

And thank you to Paul "Monkey" Whelan. That moment I returned from a trip to the US in 1989 to hear She Bangs the Drums for the first time, blasting at full whack from the room of a new, un-introduced flatmate who had moved in while I was gone remains one of the most comical and musically changing moments of my life!

A Note About Errors

It's hard enough writing a trivia quiz where the subject is in contemporary times, let alone circa 33 years ago when the brain was somewhat open to, shall we say, certain influences!

Although I fact check relentlessly, and all the info in this book is from trusted sources, clearly there is a large potential for error here. If you've spotted something that's not quite right, please let me know at the email below and I'll do my best to address it.

djmotonoir@gmail.com

Thanks!

9 798375 710174